Dedication

To

My 3 Kings in Training
Kevonte, Lonnell and Jamal

Contents

Acknowledgements

First and foremost, I would like to thank my Lord and Savior Jesus Christ for giving me the vision for this book a day before Thanksgiving in 2015. I would like to acknowledge my sisters, who for whatever reason, always believe in me when I say I am going to do something. Amanda gives her advice but always agree with all my ideas I come up with even if it's a different one every day. Kamesha is always supportive and has my back as a big sister. Keshia believes in me even if she doesn't want to. Melanie, who is my Irish, twin laughs at my ideas but tells me to go for it. Tasha always says, that "she is proud of her little sister and encourages me to keep up the good work." My mother always makes comments like, "I can't wait till you make it so you can buy me a house." I would like to thank my father "The Honorable Arthur James Stewart Jr., who thinks very highly of me and always reminds me that I am special in my own way. My only brother Sonny supports me in his own way.

I would like to give a special shout out to my 3 cousins the "Triple Threat," Ocean, Alexis and Charmaine, for their indescribable support and they believe in me more than myself at times. I would like to thank all my extended family and friends for their support. I would like to thank my grandma Lucille McMillian who holds the biggest place in my heart, and is very encouraging, loving and has been there to support me in any way that she possibly could. I would like to thank my church family and my big sister in ministry Elder Marlene Merchant who edited my book for me. I would also like to thank my Bishop Lanier C. Twyman Sr. for encouraging me to get my book out once he read the rough draft.

I would be remiss if I didn't thank my 3 Kings in training Kevonte, Lonnell and Jamal for supporting their mother in any way that they could. To my Ophthalmology Family which is what we've become One Family, One Goal, One Mission and most importantly One Team. From the Front desk Staff (Damian and Elide), All Upper Management, Staff Doctors, Residents, Enlisted, my work mother Ms. Cook, my work auntie Adele, my work sisters Kiwanda, Loretta, Tosha, Candice and last but not least all the patients who allowed me to implement this concept into the workplace to make every day at work a good day. I couldn't have done it without your encouragement and support.

Introduction

After years of being frustrated, tired and constantly disappointed by life, I decided that something needed to change. I realized that no matter which day I got paid, the salary was never enough. Although people would think that I was always happy, deep down inside something was missing. I began to wish things like, "if I had more hours, I would have more money," or "if I had a better job I could do this" and or "if the children fathers would do this I could do that." I came to the realization that if I wanted to stay happy, one it starts with me and two, it ends with me. I came to a point that once Friday drew closer, I would find myself happier than usual. I would make weekend plans and even try to invite at least one person to church.

I was looking for love in all the wrong places. I realized that getting more money wasn't going to give me what I needed. I opened my Bible to Psalm 16:11 and it reads, "You make known to me the path of life; in your presence, there is the fullness of joy; at your right hand are pleasures forevermore." The scripture alone gave me hope and reminded me that there are things that money can't buy. It is amazing how you never realize that you could very well be affected by the company you keep. I've worked since I was 12 years old and as I began to get older and more experienced, I found myself changing in a worldly manner. Monday's were frustrating, Tuesday's were annoying, Wednesday's were 2 days down and 2 days to go until' Friday, Thursday was Friday Eve and Friday was indeed a Happy Friday. I was influenced by complaining about the day of the week yet I remained happy shortly after.

I have come to the conclusion from experience that manager's matter, employees matter, the customer's matter, the company matters and everyone else who works behind the scene in the day to day operations of any business matters. If we all could be on the same page then in reality, "Team work makes the dream work!" Once I changed my perspective, my way of thinking, my attitude, my work performance and my effort, it made coming to work a lot easier. There is no better feeling in the world than to wake up and actually want to go to work knowing that you will make a difference in the workplace. I heard the old folks say, that this joy I have the world didn't give it to me and the world can't take it away. Unless you experience this joy that God can give you, then you will never really understand me. Psalm 28:7 also reminds us that, "The Lord is my strength and my shield; my heart trusted in him, and I am helped: therefore my heart rejoiceth: and with my song will I praise him." I applied the scriptures to my life and things began to change.

CHAPTER 1

Smiling Through the Rain

Would you agree that when rain is forecast, your mood tends to change? How selfish would it be for it not to rain? How would the trees grow, plants get watered, or the earth be nourished? Never looked at it that way, right? So in April 2014, I was diagnosed with sleep apnea and Narcolepsy. Deep down inside of me, I translated the doctor's report as "rain in the forecast." So I was told what needed to be done and instead of crying, I began to smile. The reason I could smile is that I knew two things: one, God is in control and two, trouble doesn't last forever.

Sleep apnea is a common disorder in which you have one or more pauses in breathing or shallow breaths while you

Sleep. Breathing pauses can last from a few seconds to minutes. Untreated sleep apnea causes a person to stop breathing repeatedly during their sleep; sometimes hundreds of time. This means that the brain and the rest of the body may not get enough oxygen. As I researched this disorder, parts of me started becoming weak, but the Holy Spirit reminded me of Galatians 6:9, that was like fire shut up in my bones to not get weary in well doing. Just in this short time, I realized that God strategically made me exactly how He wanted me to be and this doctor's appointment was simply part of my life story.

I was told or rather instructed that I would have to use a CPAP machine at night. It was very uncomfortable and annoying. CPAP means a Continuous Positive Airway Pressure therapy. The machine is used to support a patient who has obstructive sleep apnea (OSA) breathe more easily during sleep. A CPAP machine increases air pressure in your throat so that your airway doesn't collapse when you breathe in. So, as I began to go through the process, the rain began to come down a little harder. Ever heard the saying, "When it rains, it pours?"

I didn't know how serious my condition was, and I didn't take using my machine quite serious until all hell broke loose. I knew that if I failed to use the machine properly, I would not be able to wake up the next morning. It took me a whole year to understand the importance of using my machine after it caused me to lose my job. I started using the machine maybe 3 or 4 days in a week. I became a bit arrogant and told myself that if I don't wake up from not using it, then maybe it was just my time to go. Sometimes I was just

Extremely busy with my kids, sports, church activities, homework, and housework so before I could put it on I would fall asleep. I was terminated for falling asleep on the job even after providing my medical documentation. I resumed work on Sept 16 and due to improper use of the machine, it resulted in what I called the breaking point in my healing. I realized that the only way I would be healed is by following instructions because the victory is already won.

Now, Narcolepsy is a condition characterized by extreme tendency to fall asleep whenever in a relaxing surrounding. It is a neurological disorder that affects the control of sleep and wakefulness. People with narcolepsy experience excessive daytime drowsiness and intermittent, uncontrollable moments of falling asleep during the day. These sudden sleep attacks may occur during any type of activity at any time of the day. On a daily basis, I struggle with trying to stay awake at work, driving to and from work. I would even have to pull over while driving if I became sleepy. I have fallen asleep while talking to my kids, in between conversations, or just sitting down for a few minutes.

My ultimate goal is for God to work a miracle, and I will declare His mighty works. To date, I was never given medication for Narcolepsy but will continue to trust in my true and living God, who is the best physician.

Part two of the rain, on Christmas Eve of 2014, I was told that because my menstrual cycle was irregular, there was a high possibility of having a tumor on my brain. I was scheduled and had an MRI, which confirmed after several tests that I had a brain tumor on my pituitary gland.

I was not scared, but all I could say to myself was, "if it's not one thing it's another." However, no matter what, I was determined to smile and be grateful for every new day I was given. For the Bible says in Psalm 118:24, "This is the day the Lord has made; we will rejoice and be glad in it."

I was put on some medication and instructed to take it twice a week. I felt like I was being put to a test in the spirit realm and decided to trust God like never before. The doctor told me that she would see me in 3 months and I responded, "No, I am going to talk to Jesus and will be seeing you in 3 months." As my faith was tested, I began to study for my exam. I was encouraged through the scripture that God won't put more on me than I can bear. Psalm 138:3, "In the day when I cried out, you answered me, and made me bold with strength in my soul."

Chapter 1 Writing Session

Can you think of any rain in the forecast experience you've had before?

1.

2.

3.

4.

5.

CHAPTER 2

The Process

As I began to transform my thoughts, my way of thinking, and my attitude, things began to change. Everything that we go through in life must go through a process. For example: a child in their mother's womb; a caterpillar in the cocoon; a chick in an egg; snakes are always changing; becoming a doctor; an adult; transitioning from elementary school to middle school; kittens to cats; puppies to dogs; becoming a Minister of the Gospel; adopting a child; becoming a Pastor; going to school for a PhD; becoming a gourmet chef; becoming an analyst, and or your desire to one day be a judge. No matter the situation, we must not abort the process.

To convince myself on a daily basis, I had to renew my mind. On days when the sun didn't shine, I had to wear

Bright colors and be the sun. When I had more month at the end of my money, I encouraged myself that momma always said there would be days like this. Scripture reminds me in Philippians 4:19, "And my God shall supply all your needs according to His riches in glory by Christ Jesus." I had reached the point where giving up was never an option. On days when the kids were driving me crazy, I had to declare that "I can do all things through Christ who strengthens me!" When I had rough days at work, I was determined to positively turn my day around by making someone else laugh or smile.

The process of changing my days of the week to everyday being a Friday did not happen overnight. I literally became a tape recorder, and I said it to myself so many times that I actually started believing it. Have you ever heard the saying, "practice makes perfect." I had to endure, press, lift my head up, remain humble, experience heartache and above all, I had to take a stand for what I believed in. I encouraged myself that at this day; time and age I didn't leave worldly things to get saved to be sad. The devil is a liar. Scripture reminds us in Ecclesiastes 9:11, "I have seen something else under the sun: the race is not given to the swift or the battle to the strong, nor does food come to the wise or wealth to be brilliant or favor to the learned, but time and chance happen to them all."

I was so convinced that if I didn't let my emotions overtake my day that just the thought of how it could impact my workplace and others was enough to go through this process. There will be sometimes when we will not be able to take detours, shortcuts and alternate ways. Due to   the workplace being our second home, we must treat it as if we were greeting people coming to visit us, which shall push us to be pleasant, nice and spread God's love to everyone we come in contact with. It also reminded me when I began to grow dreads and had to go through the ugly stage; people kept reminding me that I had to go through the process to enjoy the full effect of having dreads. It was 12 months of encouraging myself that I could do it and that this too would soon be over. The process would not be easy but it would be worth it.

I had gotten to a point where I changed my calendar days from Monday- Friday to all Fridays and people are normally happy on Saturday and Sunday so I never had to worry about those two days. This was a challenge that I was willing to go through because my vision of making everyday a Friday was worth the struggle. Not everybody will agree with your dreams, goals, and desires, but all you truly need is enough Faith to start the process, enough Faith to go through the process and enough Faith to praise God at the beginning before the end. Have you ever heard the saying that, "anything worth having is worth waiting for?" How about, "If God brought me to it He will bring me through it?" I am glad that I made it through the process and what a blessing it is for everyday to be Friday.

Chapter 2 Writing Session

Can you recall any process that you've tried to avoid?

1.

2.

3

4.

5.

CHAPTER 3

Having a different Mindset

Matthew 15:11 "Not that which goeth into the mouth defileth a man; but that which cometh out of the mouth, this defileth a man."

While growing up, grandma would say that a mind is a terrible thing to waste. So when you are young it doesn't register but as you get older you begin to realize what grandma said was true. Everything we do, our actions, our strategies, our plans, our goals, our decision-making, and even our very next move starts in our minds, moves to our heart and eventually becomes our actions. Romans 12:2 "And do not be conformed to this world, but be transformed by the renewing of your mind, that you may prove what is that good and acceptable and perfect will of God." When God created us He made all of us in his own image and gave us all a different mindset. Your mind is not like mine nor is my mind

Like yours. Therefore, if we properly use our minds for things that are positive and this world would be a better place.

Philippians 4:8 "Finally, brethren, whatsoever things are true, whatsoever things are honest, whatsoever things are just, whatsoever things are pure, whatsoever things are lovely, whatsoever things are of good report, if there be any virtue, and if there be any praise think on these things."

The Scripture given helps to encourage and motivate us into changing our mindset to think positive. We as people, are preprogrammed and have been brainwashed into thinking things like; if it sounds really good then it's too good to be true; if something good happens then something bad is around the corner; we believe that things like if our mother or father never accomplished anything that our future is done; we often allowed people to talk negatively about us and it gets into our minds and cause us to eventually believe in a lie. I said all that to say, you are great, you are destined to be great simply because the God we serve is great. Never let negativity come between you positively being all you can be in anything you do. As it pertains to the workplace, in school, in church, school teacher, and even a principle, you will be surprised how one mindset could change the atmosphere.

For example: As I practiced and trained myself into thinking that everyday could be Friday people would tell me things like, "Don't say that Happy Friday stuff to me! "My response was simply, "until I convince you that every day could be Friday or indeed everyday could be a good day I won't stop." What I realize is that if you have a passion or doing something you love, you have to remember that not

11

Everyone will agree with you. People would also say things like, "On Friday I would be happier!" My response would be, "well you sure are dressed as if it was Friday so you could have fooled me." It was always my desire to make others smile, feel special and make every day feel like Friday. Nothing is impossible as long as you believe. The most recent comment someone made when I said, Happy Wednesday was, "Yes, 2 more days to go!" I kindly asked what day do you want to reach and she says, Friday then the weekend." Of course, I said that everyday can be Friday if that's what you want it to be and I smiled. I use to feel the same way until I changed my mindset. These are a few examples of how simply changing your mindset makes all the difference, so I challenge you that if your job is negative all the time, dealing with mean supervisors, doctors insensitive to your test results and even the co-workers that seem impossible to get along with, I am a living witness that love, plus a positive attitude can shift an atmosphere in any organization.

To be honest, you have to dare to be different at times if you want a different or unique outcome in an awkward situation. Have you ever realized that it takes more effort to lead than to be a follower? Think about it. If everybody around you thought the same and didn't desire to excel but was fine where they were it would not require much. On the other hand, if a person wants to think outside the box, desires to further their education, and or no longer want to hang around the same people it would require for him to move by simply changing his mindset. If we want to follow how anyone thinks, we might as well follow Jesus, it's a win-win situation with this option. Philippians 2:5 reads, "Let this mind be in

You, which was also in Christ Jesus." Luke 10:27 "And he answered, you shall love the Lord your God with all your heart and with all your soul and with all your strength and with your entire mind, and your neighbor as yourself." Now with this scripture, it will allow you to put not only changing your mindset but put things into perspective as it pertains to how we love God or are encouraged to do so. If we have a worldly mindset and we don't allow God to change our mind daily then we won't be able to love properly. It is very significant that we focus our thoughts and actions on him.

Romans 8:6, "For to set the mind on the flesh is death, but to set the mind on the Spirit is life and peace."

This is one of those challenging scriptures that will force you to change certain things, not have certain conversations and avoid certain actions. If we allow our heavenly Father to change our mindset, then life and peace are ours. Does it make sense to set our minds on things that are ungodly if the end result is death? It is imperative that we grasp the importance of guarding our mind, hearts, and ways. God wants what is best even for our minds but what are we willing to change to make it happen is the posing question?

Let's pray.

Lord, we come to you in Jesus name asking You to help us change our mindset; the things we lust over in thought and anything that is not of you; Father we ask for You to create in us a clean heart and renew in us the right spirit; God change our mindset to Your mindset please order our steps in Your Word and we will be careful to give You the Glory; God, w e

Thank You for moving the mountains of negative thoughts, filthy desires, and past sinful pleasures, help us to walk in the newness of a different mindset and renew it daily in Jesus most precious and wonderful name we count it done, Amen.

Chapter 3 Writing Session

Can you make a list of things you need to have a different mindset about? (Be open and honest with yourself.)

1.

2

3.

4.

5.

6.

7.

8.

9.

10.

CHAPTER 4

Every day is Payday

I know that you are thinking to yourself how in the world could every day be a payday and I was in the same boat before I discovered it. Without getting too spiritual, we are literally paid by God every day in some form or fashion. He provides everyday His mercy, grace, peace, joy, forgiveness, humility, love, kindness, a clear mind, activity of our limbs, food, shelter, clothing, patience, long-suffering, and most importantly He gave Jesus.

For the Bible says, while we were yet sinners that Christ died for us. It also says that if we ask it shall be given, if we seek we shall find and if we knock, the door shall be opened. (Matthew 7:7)The truth of the matter is that you will not be able to monetarily get paid every day but we must learn how to be content with all that God has already given you. We

Take too much for granted as people, but if we could change our perspective and our way of thinking then every day could be payday.

For instance, on Monday we will get a check for Mercy, Tuesday for Grace, Wednesday for Strength, Thursday for Prosperity, Friday for Motivation, Saturday for a reasonable amount of health and Sunday a check for Hope. It all begins in our minds, it moves to our heart and it eventually becomes manifested in our actions. In order to move we should not take the little things for granted, but to truly consider how in whatever state we are to be content. Philippians 4:11 reads, "I am not saying this because I am in need, for I have learned to be content whatever the circumstances." I will cover Mercy, Forgiveness, and Grace, which I believe are three benefits that we either take for granted or don't fully comprehend.

Mercy

Mercy is compassion or forgiveness shown towards someone whom it is within one's power to punish or harm. God truly does not treat us as our sins deserve and because He loves us, He renews our mercy daily. Lamentations 3:22-23 reads; 22 – "Through the Lord's mercies we are not consumed because His compassions fail not." 23 – "They are new every morning; great is your faithfulness." As a mother, I have to show mercy to my children at times only because of how grateful I am for my mother, grandmother and the Lord for showing me mercy when it could have been the other way.

17

Has your back ever been up against the wall? Have you ever experienced being in between a rock and a hard place? Ever been laid off from a job at the beginning of the month? Have you experienced losing a loved one during or after the holidays? Do you recall almost losing your mind after your divorce? Have you ever been hungry and your freezer was empty? So every question I posed was an example of God providing peace in the midst of the storm.

There is a peace that is indescribable and it can only come from one source. Philippians 4:7 reminds us of God's peace. It reads, "And the peace of God, which passeth all understanding, shall keep your hearts and minds through Christ Jesus."

Have you ever imagined how it would be if you didn't have a sound mind? Could you imagine having to take medication just to have temporary peace, to relax your nerves and or to calm you down from being angry? The peace of God can get you through those times you thought were impossible. God's peace is the kind you have when you are told to leave everything behind, and God guarantees you that everything is going to be alright.

In Genesis 12:1, The Lord had said to Abram, "Go from your country, your people and your father's household to the land I will show you." This scripture shows that although Abram had no idea of what was going on and or what to expect, through God he had peace.

Forgiveness

Forgiveness teaches us to stop feeling anger towards someone who has done something wrong: to stop blaming (someone): to stop feeling angry about (something): to forgive someone for (something wrong) according to Merriam Webster. Forgiveness is a payday that we receive daily. At times, I don't think we fully grasp how much we have been forgiven. Either we will learn how to forgive willingly or our Father in heaven will not forgive us. We must realize that forgiveness is never for the other person but it is for us. I know you are wondering why, so let me help you. I will not tell you that you will go to sleep at night and then wake up able to forgive any and everybody, but like I mentioned in Chapter 2, we must not abort the process. I will cover forgiving people, ourselves and a thorough understanding of God's forgiveness that is offered to us.

Matthew 6:14-15, "For if you forgive other people when they sin against you, your heavenly Father will also forgive you. But if you do not forgive others their sins, your Father will not forgive your sins." Let's walk through the text together; For if you forgive other people when they sin against you: People are going to disappoint you, wrong you, lie to you, take you for granted, step on your toes, stab you in the back and the whole nine yards. What you have to do is focus on pleasing God and allowing the love you have for God to strengthen you to forgive. This part of our walk with Christ is a mandate and not an option. The Scripture goes on to say, your heavenly Father will also forgive you. Could you imagine where we would be if our sins were not

Forgiven? Check this out, all the wrong you have done, people you have hurt, lies you have told, toes you have stepped on and even the ones you love the most who you have wronged and God forgave you. I don't know about you, but I know that I have not always been so good and God is still perfecting forgiveness in me today so I offer forgiveness to all because of it. Next the scripture says, But if you do not forgive others their sins: if you hold grudges, not talk to people and completely dismiss them because of their sins, just look in the mirror because you will reap what you sow Not forgiving blocks your blessings and it discontinues the overflow that God promises us when we don't walk in it.

1 John 1:9, "If we confess our sins, he is faithful and just and will forgive us our sins and purify us from all unrighteousness." Walk with me down memory lane, because there was a time when I was scared to confess my sins to God. If we confess our sins: this is the next step in maturing in your walk with God. You have learned to forgive others and now you must forgive yourself and not walk around in condemnation. There is no sin too big or small for God to forgive; all He requires is that we ask. This is also not a free ticket to sin and I just thought I would add that. Next it says, he is faithful and just and will forgive us our sins and to purify us from all unrighteousness: so not only is he faithful and just on top of that he is the only one who can forgive us of our sins, not Buddha, not Muhammad, not Confucius, not even the Priest can forgive us. Then, He is able to purify us from all unrighteousness. Purify further means to be decontaminated. Meaning, when we are washed with Jesus blood we go from unrighteous to righteous in him. Psalm

51:10 is a daily eye opener that we need the Lord every day and the process never stops. It says, "Create in me a clean heart, O God; and renew a right spirit within me." Never stop repenting and confessing your shortcomings to a true and living God who is always available, willing and able.

Colossians 1:13-14 God rescued us from dead-end alleys and dark dungeons. He's set us up in the kingdom of the Son He loves so much, the Son who got us out of the pit we were in, got rid of the sins we were doomed to keep repeating. I will need your help to walk through this; God rescued us from dead-end alleys and dark dungeons. So I used the message Bible version so that it could be broken down into lowest terms. We must not forget all that God has done for us and how far He has brought us. I don't know about you, but He has kept me in the midst of storms, allowed me to survive car accidents, He has provided a way out with me when dealing with crazy men and most of all I was blind and now I see. The remaining of the scriptures says He's set us up in the kingdom of the Son he loves so much: Because he loves us he gave his only begotten son to die for us and promises us eternal life through His Son. Furthermore the scripture ends by saying the Son who got us out of the pit we were in, got rid of the sins we were doomed to keep repeating: So we were literally sinking in sin seeking to rise no more and God came and snatched us out of the hand of the enemy, died for our sins on Calvary although He knew we were bound to still fall after being forgiven. I don't know about you but that is good news to me and a true definition of God's love for his children. I am ever so grateful for all the forgiveness that has been shown to me so I seek to do the

Same in return so that my father in heaven may be glorified.

Grace

Grace means to get something that you do not deserve, unmerited favor. If you live long enough you will begin to recognize the favor that is upon your life. I don't know about you but there was a time that I know I wasn't qualified for a position yet God open the door of grace and gave me the opportunity. Not just me but some of you are experiencing living in houses you don't deserve, cars you never thought you would have, children are receiving unusual recognition, you are being chosen over people who are more educated than you, the doctor said that you were going to make it yet, the Lord spared your life, your business has been growing out of nowhere, you got a husband or a wife you know you didn't deserve, your credit score is the highest it's ever been in your life, pulls us from the back of the line and brings us to the front and overall grace has afforded us many chances to get it right although we didn't deserve it. Grace saved us and grace keep us humble.

Ephesians 2:8-9 [8] "For it is by grace you have been saved, through faith—and this is not from yourselves, it is the gift of God— [9] not by works so that no one can boast. So this particular scripture reminds in the very beginning how we were saved; it is written that, for it is by grace you have been saved." We do not have to second-guess how or why we were saved because God makes it plain and clear that although none of us deserved to be saved, it was the benefit of God's grace that we have been saved and nothing else. Then it helps us to hold onto our faith a little stronger and says, through

Faith and this is not from you: The faith that we have in Jesus Christ helps us to accept being saved by grace. Which means, we can be given the opportunity to accept Jesus and the only way it can be sealed is by Faith? The end of verse 8 into 9 says, it is the gift of God-not by works, so that no one can boast: In lowest terms you cannot do anything to make God save you, but it is clear as clear can get that we are saved by grace through faith and it is God's gift to us not our gift to him.

Humility is something that is gained and practiced as we grow in wisdom and grace. Biblically speaking, humility is the opposite of pride. And according to one thesaurus source, some other antonyms for humility are arrogance, assertiveness, egoism, pretentiousness, and self- importance. Proverbs 11:2, "When pride comes, then comes disgrace, but with humble is wisdom. When pride comes, then comes disgrace:" We have to be careful that we don't try to take God's credit when we are blessed beyond measure and know that is was only because of His grace. Pride gets in the way of gratefulness and leads to ungratefulness by way of disgrace. The next part goes to say that, but with humble is wisdom: The significance in this text is an indication of God making a declaration about something and in this case, it was if you remain humble it will result in wisdom.

The songwriter has a song called Amazing Grace and I provide you the lyrics:

Amazing Grace, How sweet the sound that saved a wretch like me. I once was lost, but now am found, was blind but now I see. T'was grace that taught my heart to fear. And grace my fears relieved. How precious did that Grace appear, the hour I first believed? Through many dangers, toils, and snares, I have already come; this grace has brought me safe

Thus far and grace will lead me home. The Lord has promised well to me. His work my hopes secure; He will my shield and portion be, as long as life endures. Yea, when this flesh and heart shall fail, and mortal life shall cease; I shall possess within the veil, a life of joy and peace. When we've been here ten thousand years bright shining as the sun. We've no fewer days to sing God's praise than when we've first begun. Copyright

Chapter 4 Writing Session

What are some ways God has paid you this week?

1.

2.

3.

4.

5.

List 10 things that made you smile today, that could have only been blessing from God.

1.

2.

3.

4.

5.

6.

7.

8.

9.

10.

CHAPTER 5

Try something new

I've noticed that when people want something new that's tangible they don't mind going the extra mile. However, I've noticed when people have to try something new that will bring about change that is not tangible, but physically, emotionally and can result in opposition or opportunity, it develops hesitation and procrastination. Hesitation is the action of pausing or hesitating before saying or doing something. Often times when we have to try something new, we pause to think about three things: how will it affect me, how will it affect others and would I rather continue to do what I am used to just in case I don't like the outcome? Procrastination is the action of delaying or postponing something. As it pertains to trying something new we will postpone things such as making a commitment, agreeing to contracts and even applying for another job only because we

Are so used to the one we are at even when we are unhappy. It is impossible for us to live and not experience something new because it's bound to come with both age and time.

Growing up as a child in your school days, did your teacher try something new? Whether it was a new way to teach, a different way of testing or she broke down a math problem and made your life a lot easier. As a teacher, you always have to try something new because depending on whom you teach; you must be creative knowing that people learn differently. As you continue to grow, but not actually adulthood, you must journey through the adolescent stage in which you will be required to try something new. Prior to becoming a full-fledged adult, you may run into things like peer-pressure, bullying, being the class clown, and finding yourself and even being called the teacher 's pet. Now all except being a bully I've experienced, nevertheless there came a point in life where I had to try something n e w .

Peer pressure brought about me smoking weed; being the class clown was something I did because I always got jokes, finding myself was something I had to do once becoming pregnant in 10th grade; and because of my integrity in school was called the teacher's pet. Once I got older, peer-pressure no longer was successful; being the class clown was no longer popular and because I was a mom I simply began to look at things from a different perspective. As an adult trying something new could go a number of different ways. You can be forced to try something new, you can be led to try something new and life happens and trying something new, comes along with the change.

When you are forced to try something new it requires immediate change; you're shocked or all of a sudden something happens. For example: when you have an unexpected car accident and your car is a total loss and now you have to catch the train for a few weeks. It is the 21st century and you haven't caught the train in years, but you are now being forced to try something new. As you become a mature Christian, you are led to try something new as it pertains to your life, how you live and your lifestyle. God has a way of leading us into doings things to better the kingdom, our spiritual well-being and individually. An example of change happening all of a sudden is when the doctors tell you that you have a tumor on your brain and they have to conduct immediate surgery today.

In the beginning when I felt like I wanted to make a change on my job, which would require me to try something new, besides me being the new kid on the block, I did not think it was possible. I have to admit that doubt came first, fear came second and worrying tried to stop me from the start. However, I realized even as a child that I was unique and set apart so I took this thought and run with it. You must believe in yourself when no one thinks it's possible, when your ideas don't make sense to you and when you clearly have no clue what will come along with the change. We as of people all have something that we have run away from, avoided when we were younger and ever tried to escape all because of the fear of trying something new. I heard the old folks say that "there is nothing wrong change as long as you are changing for the better."

John 20:29 Then Jesus told him, "Because you have

Seen me, you believed; blessed are those who have not seen me and yet have believed."

Doubt is that little thought in your head where you criticize and try to convince yourself into thinking you don't qualify for the position. Doubt tries to discourage you of even proceeding with the thought. Doubting yourself discredits your gifts and talents that God has bestowed upon you and enables you to operate in your gift. We must remove doubt and replace it with Hope. Doubt according to Google is a feeling of uncertainty or lack of conviction.

1 John 4:18 "There is no fear in love. But perfect love drives out fear because fear has to do with punishment, the one who fears are made perfect in love."

Fear is the thought that triggers from doubt in which it makes you feel that you will fail as in the past. Fear is truly not of God and a form of distraction to you so that we won't rely on God's power but our own. Fear has to be replaced with the Faith that we have in Jesus Christ. Knowing that we can do all things through Christ is the recipe to transforming the fear that we use into the Faith that we have now. Fear according to Google is an unpleasant emotion caused by the belief that someone or something is dangerous, likely to cause pain or a threat.

John 14:27 "Peace I leave with you; my peace I give you. I do not give to you as the world gives. Do not let your hearts be troubled and do not be afraid."

Worrying simply is a stronghold between you and yourself which deceives us to still try to fix something that

God has already worked out. Worrying is due to a lack of worshipping in which our focus is temporarily on the problem instead of the problem solver. Worrying was telling me that because of all I was currently facing how could I truly be happy and still worship in the midst of it all. I tend to feel like David from time to time when he said in Psalm 34: "I will bless the Lord at all times: his praise shall continually be in my mouth." I simply took this scripture and ran with it. I was determined that I would be the change in the workplace that I wanted to see. There is nothing better than following your heart by trying something new and seeing your ideas manifest right before your eyes. Worrying according to Google is causing anxiety about actual or potential problems.

Chapter 5 Writing Session

"Can you name at least three new things you had to try?"

1.

2.

3.

CHAPTER 6

Dealing with Multiple Attitudes

There are all kinds of people in the world today, which typically will result in dealing with multiple attitudes. We all have different lifestyles, drive different cars, have different families, different careers, different religions and like I said in the previous chapter, a different mindset. I believe there are four specific areas that need to be perfect in order for one to be equipped in dealing with multiple attitudes. We as people fall into one of the four categories; we lack discipline, we don't understand the power of words, we must learn to love the way God loves and we have to know the difference between being offensive and being objective. How in the world could every day be Friday for Meyana having to deal with multiple attitudes?

Lack of discipline

Proverbs 25:28

"He that hath no rule over his own spirit is like a city that is broken down, and without walls."

There is nothing wrong with lacking discipline in certain areas; however, once you are not able to admit you lack discipline is where the problem begins. I will give you a couple of areas in which I use to lack discipline. We all at some point in our lives will lack discipline. Now I can only speak for myself, but there was a time where I lacked discipline with spending money. I would find myself not happy unless I spent all that I had. I was so broke I couldn't pay attention, robbing Martha to pay Mary and maxing out my credit cards. I didn't realize that I would need to save money for a rainy day until the rain came and my account was overdrawn. Once I was able to admit I had a problem was when I went to the problem solver and was given a plan to get out. We also lack discipline in our eating habits. Again, I can only speak for myself on this note.

So I will make this short and sweet; I had a serious problem of over eating in which I developed "BED" Binge Eating Disorder. No, I was never diagnosed with it, but I use to fry and bake chicken at the same time at 12:00 midnight. I would eat until I felt sick. I was eating my problems away instead of praying. I finally realized that I had a problem when the scale said one hundred ninety-six pounds and my jean size went from 8 to 14. I began to watch how and what I ate, exercised and developed discipline in this specific area.

Last, but not least, I used to lack discipline in my daily devotions which included reading the Word and praying to God on a consistent basis. There is nothing worse than a Christian who knows what to do, how to do it, yet it has nothing to do with their lifestyle, how they are living or their life.

I can remember when my pastor preached a sermon about "How to get my joy back" and while he preached it, I realized that because I was spiritually malnourished the enemy crept into my life, stole my joy, peace, and happiness and devotion time. So I had to be intentional in getting my joy back and reconnecting with God. So with regards to lacking discipline in certain areas, I overall had to become efficient in dealing with multiple attitudes. I've learned that no matter how bad of a day a person is having, you can control the outcome which I'll explain in my topic on "the power of words."

Power of Words

Proverbs 18:21 "Death and life are in the power of the tongue: and they that love it shall eat the fruit thereof."

In today's society, people don't realize that words matter. Back in the day and I am only 31, people use to say, "Sticks and stones may break my bones but words will never hurt me." I've noticed growing up that words hurt, words damage and words can ruin your life or make your life better. On a daily basis, I had to realize that my words could make a person better or I could contribute to making their life worse. There is so much power in our words, but what we choose to do with them makes all the difference.

34

As a mother of 3 boys, I was not always so careful about the words I chose and know that I said something's that was not pleasing to them, myself and most importantly God. I read a book titled, "Power of Words" by Shawn McBride and it changed my mind and perspective on how much power our words carry.

I also read a book entitled, "31 Promises to Speak over Your Life" by Joel Osteen and it shifted my prayers, made me see myself differently and created a deeper desire to seek God's face and will for my life. It's nothing wrong with encouraging someone you don't know, praying for someone you know in need, putting others before yourself, being slow to speak but always ready for reconciliation and if you don't have anything positive to say don't say nothing at all. I encourage you, moving forward, to speak life and not death.

Learning to Love Right

1 Corinthians 13:4-8 "Love is patient, love is kind. It does not envy, it does not boast, it is not proud. It does not dishonor others, it is not self-seeking, it is not easily angered, it keeps no record of wrongs, and Love does not delight in evil but rejoices with the truth. It always protects, always trusts always hope, always preserves, Love never fails. But where there are tongues, they will be stilled: where there is knowledge, it will pass away."

The Bible commands us to love everybody, honor our mothers and fathers, for husbands to love their wives as Christ loved the church, for wives to be submissive to their own husbands and for us to even love those who cursed us.

All of these examples are an expression which demonstrates the Love one has for one another. There is nowhere in the Bible where it says that we're all born lovable because we are all uniquely different. However, whether a person is loveable or not should not dictate whether or not you love them.

There are three main points to learning how to love right. First, we must love God, love ourselves the way God loves us and then love our neighbor as thy self. Loving God would be us doing things such as: keeping his commandments, studying his word, praying to him and fulfilling his purpose in our lives. People always say things like, "God knows my heart," "God will forgive me," and even "I'm not God so I don't have to love everyone." When we are truly in love with God, nobody has to beg you to attend church, pay you to serve, convince you to give, dare you to pray, award you to study and or challenge you to sin less these things come automatically.

Secondly learning to love ourselves the way God loves us. Just because you've tried to convince yourself that you love yourself doesn't mean that you actually believe it to be true. We have all done something's we are ashamed of, secrets we will never tell and even look at ourselves in the mirror and don't like what we see. We have to be aware that God's love for us goes beyond our faults.

Jesus was sent to die for our sins and there is nothing that we can do to separate us from the God's love. Romans 8:37-39 "Yet in all these things we are more than conquerors through Him who loved us, for I am persuaded that neither death, nor life, nor angels, nor principalities, nor powers, nor

Things present nor things to come, nor height nor depths, nor any other created thing, shall be able to separate us from the love of God which is in Christ Jesus our Lord." We have to speak life, into our lives and know that we are fearfully and wonderfully made. For it is written Psalm 139:14 "I will praise you, for I am fearfully and wonderfully made, marvelous are your works, and that my soul knows very well.

We are a royal priesthood and a chosen generation." For it is also written, 1 Peter 2:9 "But ye are a chosen generation, a royal priesthood, a holy nation, a peculiar people; that ye should shew forth the praises of him who hath called you out of darkness into His marvelous light." We must forgive ourselves, acknowledge our uniqueness and walk in God's unusual favor that is upon our lives.

Last but not least once you have mastered loving God, loving yourself than you can move into loving our neighbor as thyself. There are a lot of things that can be Conquered through love. Your mean boss needs love; confusion in the home, put some loves on it, your marriage having problems, put some love on it. This world would truly be a better place if we learn to love and realize that we all will fall short, we all will make mistakes and we won't always agree, but it should never supersede our love for one another.

We have to get to the point where spreading God's love to all people is the trending topic. It pleases God when we see about the poor, encourage the broken-hearted, speak life into the prostitutes, give hope to the drug dealers, give your cousin on drugs a hug instead of a lecture, open the door for the elderly and or go out of your way to do w e l l

Deed for a stranger, but most importantly chooses to love God and the people of God on purpose.

"The difference between being offensive and being objective"

In the world today people often view themselves as something to hate on, and somebody that everybody wants to be like which ultimately results in a person becoming offensive versus objective. The more love we have for one another the less offensive we will become and be objective when conversing daily. To be offensive is to become offended and feel as though what someone said they were trying to hurt you. To be objective is to view the comment clearly and not bias about what was said and looking at it from their point of view.

Often times when dealing with multiple attitudes in the workplace I had to be sure not to quickly become offensive and be objective when dealing with angry patients, patients with disorders, a patient who didn't speak back and those who were telling stories about their appointment time. It was imperative that I allowed the love I have for all people to ease my daily workflow while dealing with all kinds of personalities. If and when I had to converse with a patient who was unruly, instead of stirring up anger or adding fuel to the fire, I would kindly put myself in their shoes, say some kind words, crack a joke and look at the situation objectively.

I would ask myself questions like, how do I know what kind of night they had? Do I know how their commute was?

What if I was dealing with a health issue? Would I be frustrated if I had to walk around for a few miles due to construction before I could make it to my appointment? I've learned that just because people don't agree with everything I say is not a reason to be offended but a wakeup call that I won't always agree with them either. Sometimes you've got to agree to disagree and change the subject. We as believers have to be careful not to miss an opportunity to minister to someone who is in need. We must not be controlled by our emotions because if we do it can very well hinder what God is trying to do in and through us individually and collectively. I cannot promise you that dealing with people on a daily basis is easy but once you learn love right then you can love people right where they are without a wall due to race, ethnic background or status. The bottom line is love conquerors all.

Chapter 6 Writing Session

1. Did you find this chapter helpful? Why or why not?
2. Do you feel that you are learning to love people God's way? Why or why not?
3. "How do you handle multiple attitudes? Is it hard? Why or why not?

"Can you think of at least 5 difficult attitudes that you had to encounter just this week?"

1.

2.

3.

4.

5.

CHAPTER 7

Practice what you preach

Practicing what you preach is a cliché that is abused and often misused. I am in the world but not of the world. So, I had put myself to the test, passed it and found a way to do the same thing for someone else. The name of the test was Class 101-90 day drill. Life is a precious gift from God, and he gave us his best gift which was his son Jesus Christ. An example of God demonstrating his Love towards us is in Romans 5:8, "But God commendeth his love toward us, while we were yet sinners Christ died for us." This was literally God preaching in action.

It all began in Sept 16-Dec 16. I told myself that I would test my own product on me to make sure it would work and also to ensure that I would be able to convince other people how it works. On a daily basis when I woke

41

Up, I had to look in the mirror and tell myself that today would be a good day all because "Every day is Friday!" I began to experience more happiness than ever before. I smiled on Monday, showed up early on Tuesday, I worshiped on Wednesday, Thursday I testified and on Friday was a cool breeze all because I had 72 hours to myself.

As I began to experience God's Love, Joy, Peace, and Happiness and show mercy to people, I became contagious in a good way. Contagious is the communication of disease from one person to another by close contact. Practicing what you preach can be done a number of different ways. However, I was persuaded that with my positive attitude, the love of Christ living inside of me and my desire to change my atmosphere that every day, in fact, could be Friday. You can be contagious in one or two ways; either positively or negatively. The scripture clearly identifies a child of God by the love one has for one another. From my perspective, it is becoming his disciple and being contagious in a good way. It is kind of hard to be mean or rude to a person who is nice and loving. Would you agree? Have you ever experienced being waited on by a mean waitress but her attitude changes because your attitude is pleasant? We have to get to the point where we realize that our daily actions should be a reflection of God. We not only represent God but our church family, biological family, our spiritual covering and our children as well if you are a parent.

I was not only happy because of the day of the week, but just simply the opportunity of just waking up the next day. I believe that it's not about the day of the week but what you do with your days is what really matters.

When talking to patients at work I would reply, "I am doing great because every day is Friday to me." They would reply "That's a great way to think and or I will have to take that with me." What a blessing to see fruit from your concept and making a positive impact in the workplace. For John 13:35 says, "By this, all people will know that you are my disciples if you have a love for one another."

Every so often when I have experienced going into different stores be it clothing, food, gas station or through the mall, I always feel in some stores that something was missing. Have you ever been told to leave your problems from home at home? Often times I feel like too many people are to come into the workplace with a clouded mind, not enough sleep, horrible with time management and our lack of budget planning gets us off on the wrong foot before we even began our 8 hour shift. With this concept of every day being Friday, I am convinced that no matter what we encounter, go through the night before and even rush hour traffic in the morning our work day will be like no other. Do you know what would happen to the workplace if everybody came to work happy? Do you think that businesses grow with bad customer service and rude employees? Have you ever heard that it starts from the top? I also believe that if our managers and supervisors were more pleasant, it would make the employees want to come to work, they won't call out as much and be early instead of late. Too often in the workplace, I think that upper management's negativity impacts the employees and set the wrong atmosphere for the working day. As I close this chapter, if you are in any position of leadership ask yourself this question:

How effective could a workplace be if the managers are as unhappy as the employees? What can we do to be on one accord?

Testimonials

One morning I spoke to a lady at my job, and I said, "Happy Friday" she said what do you mean "Every day is Friday." It was at that point that I realize how big this could be, how many people I could help and or what this could potentially do in the workplace. So I encourage any authors, business owners, managers, parents, Pastors, Bishops and any form of leadership we must Practice what we preached and we shall not preach what we haven't practiced.

For two weeks Dr. Brett Smith from the Ophthalmology Department where I work would come in and beat me with saying, "Happy Monday, Happy Tuesday, Happy Wednesday, Happy Thursday and Happy Friday" and it was that moment where I witness lives being changed and the positive energy transferring from me to other people.

Patients would come week after week and no matter what day of the week it was they would address me by saying, "Happy Friday!" I was so blessed to see that people no longer cared about what day of the week it was but they were simply happy to be greeted with a warm welcome.

In September of 2016 the Department Head of the Ophthalmology Department Dr. McClellan changed my name to "Miss Friday" and from that day forward that is the name that I went by. Whether throughout the weekday, on the weekend or ordering food where I had to give a name no longer did I use Meyana but I went by Miss Friday. My job loved me so much that Friday's were dedicated to me.

Chapter 7 Writing Session

Can you write down any experience that you had to practice before you could preach it?

1.

2.

3.

4.

5.

CHAPTER 8

Positive Thinking Quotes

- ❖ Nothing is good or bad, but thinking MAKES IT SO. ~William Shakespeare
- ❖ Great minds discuss ideas; Average minds discuss events; Small minds discuss people. ~Eleanor Roosevelt
- ❖ So of cheerfulness or a good temper, the more it is spent, the more of it remains. ~Ralph Waldo Emerson
- ❖ Though we travel the world over to find the beautiful, we must carry it with us or we find it not. ~Ralph Waldo Emerson
- ❖ People only see what they are prepared to see. ~Ralph Waldo Emerson

- ❖ The positive thinker sees the invisible, feels the intangible, and achieves the impossible. ~Winston Churchill

- ❖ Speaking for myself, I am an optimist - it does not seem to be much use being anything else. ~Winston Churchill

- ❖ A pessimist sees the difficulty in every opportunity; an optimist sees the opportunity in every   difficulty. ~Winston Churchill

- ❖ I have become my own version of an optimist. If I can't make it through one door, I'll go through another door - or I'll make a door. Something terrific will come no matter how dark the   present. ~Rabindranath Tagore

- ❖ Once you replace negative thoughts with positive ones, you'll start having positive results. ~Willie Nelson (American country singer)

- ❖ When I hear somebody sigh, "Life is hard," I am always tempted to ask, "Compared to   what?" ~Sydney Harris

- ❖ When you get into a tight place and everything goes against you, till it seems as though you could not hold on a minute longer, never give up then, for that is just the place and time that the tide will turn. ~Harriet Beecher Stowe

- ❖ The habit of looking on the bright side of every event is worth more   than a   thousand pounds a   year. ~Samuel Johnson

- ❖ There are always flowers for those who want to see them. ~Henri Matisse

❖ I have had dreams and I have had nightmares, but I have conquered my nightmares because of my dreams. ~Dr. Jonas Salk

❖ Keep your face to the sunshine and you cannot see the shadow. ~Helen Keller

❖ Wherever you go, no matter what the weather, always bring your own sunshine. ~Anthony J. D'Angelo

❖ We must accept finite disappointment, but we must never lose infinite hope. ~Martin Luther King, Jr.

❖ Pessimism never won any battle. ~Dwight D. Eisenhower

❖ The World is what we think it is. If we can change our thoughts, we can change the world. ~H.M. Tomlinson

❖ If you think about disaster, you will get it. Brood about death and you hasten your demise. Think positively and masterfully, with confidence and faith, and life becomes more secure, more fraught with action, richer in achievement and experience. ~Swami Vivekananda

❖ Every day may not be good, but there's something good in every day. ~Author Unknown

❖ Some of the world's greatest feats were accomplished by people not smart enough to know they were impossible. ~Doug Larson

❖ A loving person lives in a loving world. A hostile person lives in a hostile world. Everyone you meet is your mirror. ~Ken Keyes, Jr.

❖ We do not see things as they are. We see them as we are. ~Talmud

❖ He who limps is still walking. ~Stanislaw J. Lec

- A pessimist is one who makes difficulties of his opportunities and an optimist is one who makes opportunities of his difficulties. ~Harry Truman
- Act as if it were impossible to fail. ~Dorothy Broude
- Don't judge each day by the harvest you reap, but by the seeds you plant. ~Robert Louis Stevenson
- "Keep your face to the sunshine and you cannot see a shadow." ~Helen Keller
- "Once you replace negative thoughts with positive ones, you'll start having positive results." ~Willie Nelson
- "Yesterday is not ours to recover, but tomorrow is ours to win or lose." ~Lyndon B. Johnson
- "In order to carry a positive action, we must develop here a positive vision." ~Dalai Lama
- "I always like to look on the optimistic side of life, but I am realistic enough to know that life is a complex matter." ~Walt Disney
- "Positive thinking will let you do everything better than negative thinking will." ~Zig Ziglar
- "Pessimism leads to weakness, optimism to power." ~William James
- "You can't make positive choices for the rest of your life without an environment that makes those choices easy, natural, and enjoyable." ~Deepak Chopra
- "The thing that lies at the foundation of positive change, the way I see it, is service to a fellow human being." ~Lee Lacocca
- "Positive thinking is more than just a tagline. It changes the way we behave. And I firmly believe that when I am positive, it not only makes me better, but

HOW EVERYDAY CAN BE FRIDAY

It also makes those around me better." ~Harvey
Mackay

❖ "In every day, there are 1,440 minutes. That means we
have 1,440 daily opportunities to make a positive
impact." ~Les Brown

❖ "I'm a very positive thinker, and I think that is what
helps me the most in difficult moments." ~Roger
Federer

❖ "Perpetual optimism is a force multiplier." ~Colin
Powell

❖ "Attitude is a little thing that makes a big difference."
~Winston Churchill

❖ "Being miserable is a habit; being happy is a habit,
and the choice is yours." ~ Tom Hopkins

❖ "You cannot tailor-make the situations in life but you
can tailor-make the attitudes to fit those situations." ~
Zig Ziglar

❖ "Things turn out best for the people who make the
best of the way things turnout." ~John Wooden

❖ "We can't escape pain; we can't escape the essential
nature of our lives. But we do have a choice. We can
give in and relent, or we can fight, persevere, and
create a life worth living, a noble life. Pain is a fact;
our evaluation of it is a choice." ~ Jacob Held

❖ "Each problem has hidden in it an opportunity so
powerful that it literally dwarfs the problem. The
greatest success stories were created by people who
recognized a problem and turned it into an
opportunity." ~ Joseph Sugarman

- ❖ "The greatest discovery of all time is that a person can change his future by merely changing his attitude." ~ Oprah Winfrey
- ❖ "The day is what you make it! So why not make it a great one?" ~ Steve Schulte
- ❖ "Write it on your heart that every day is the best day in the year." ~ Ralph Waldo Emerson
- ❖ Philippians 4:8 "Finally, brothers, whatever is true, whatever is honorable, whatever is just, whatever is pure, whatever is lovely, whatever is commendable, if there is any excellence, if there is anything worthy of praise, think about these things."
- ❖ Proverbs 17:22 "A joyful heart is good medicine, but a crushed spirit dries up the bones."
- ❖ Hebrews 13:5 "So we can confidently say, "The Lord is my helper; I will not fear; what can man do to me?"
- ❖ Romans 8:28 "And we know that for those who love God all things work together for good, for those who are called according to his purpose."
- ❖ Philippians 4:6 "Do not be anxious about anything, but in everything by prayer and supplication with thanksgiving let your requests be made known to God."
- ❖ Philippians 4:13 "I can do all things through him who strengthens me."

Chapter 8 Writing Session

Can you create up your own positive quotes that you would like to pass onto your children or any quotes you remember that helped you along the way?

1.

2.

3.

4.

5.

Made in the USA
Columbia, SC
18 July 2021